SUPPORTED SELF-STUDY

An Introduction for Teachers

Philip Waterhouse
Project Co-ordinator

NATIONAL COUNCIL FOR EDUCATIONAL TECHNOLOGY

Published and distributed by the
National Council for Educational Technology
3 Devonshire Street, London W1N 2BA

© Council for Educational Technology 1988

First published 1988
Reprinted 1989 twice

ISBN 0 86184-177-8

NOTE: *In April 1988, the National Council for Educational Technology was formed from the merger of the Microelectronics Education Support Unit with the Council for Educational Technology.*

British Library Cataloguing in Publication Data

Waterhouse, Philip
    Supported self-study: an introduction for teachers.
    1. Independent study
    I. Title
    371.3'943   LB1049

    ISBN 0-86184-177-8

Typeset by WHM Photosetting, Greenwich, SE10 8NW

Printed in Great Britain by
BPCC Wheatons Ltd, Exeter

Contents

During the period 1979 to 1981, the Council for Educational Technology carried out a number of investigations in order to find out how new learning systems and technology might contribute to the current problems of secondary schools. It was felt that, at least for the older students, there was much to be learned from the rapid developments in Open Learning in adult and further education.

As a result of these enquiries, CET set up its Supported Self-Study Project in 1981. Three distinct phases can be recognised:

Phase 1 (1981-1983) — further investigation into current practice and experience in systems of independent learning.

Phase 2 (1983-1985) — intensive trials in a number of selected secondary schools, in order to add to the stock of experience.

Phase 3 (1985-1988) — support for local authority development programmes in Supported Self-Study.

The Project has been fortunate in that its activities coincided with a number of government initiatives on the curriculum and assessment. These have stressed the need to develop young people's personal capabilities and sense of responsibility. As a result, there is a climate of acceptance for systems which aim to design educational experiences with responsibility and active involvement as major objectives.

At the present time, a number of local authorities have development programmes in action. Some have been able to arrange secondment of teachers to support the schools and others have set up centres where the work is given priority. CET is in constant touch with those who are involved and helps with INSET events and by making training materials available.

Supported Self-Study is being used throughout the secondary age range. With the younger students, it is a natural continuation of the best primary school practice. For the older students, it serves as a preparation for the Open Learning opportunities they will meet in further education and in their working lives.

A distinctive emphasis separates Supported Self-Study from many of the previous initiatives in independent learning. This is the supreme importance given to the work of tutoring in small groups. It is through the guidance and support given in the tutorial that young people begin to acquire the habits and techniques of the independent learner. Of course, resources are also important but *by themselves* are not likely to bring about the desired changes. Supported Self-Study emphasises the crucial role of tutoring and of the management of the whole experience.

This guide book is aimed at those teachers who may be approaching Supported Self-Study for the first time. It shows how a simple trial can be conducted and provides further reference about techniques and some of the possible areas of application.

Part 1

PRINCIPLES OF SUPPORTED SELF-STUDY

Why are you interested in the shift towards more student-centred learning?

Most likely you will reply that you believe that education is not just about filling heads with knowledge. It should have much wider aims. You want your students to think for themselves, to be more active in their work, to take greater responsibility. In other words, you are more concerned with the virtue of the approach rather than the necessity for it. So let's talk about *virtue*.

VIRTUE

For the teachers who believe in it, Supported Self-Study has four main virtues:

1. It helps students to be more active in their learning. They become more involved intellectually and learn how to support and work with each other. They learn more this way and it is a more adult way of working.

2. It helps students to accept greater responsibility for their own learning. They learn to make decisions and choices for themselves, but in a thoroughly rational and responsible way, not in a childish and wilful way. Of course, this is a progressive training, not an instant declaration of autonomy for them. Many are not ready for responsibility and they have to be carefully weaned from their dependence on the teacher. But we must get started early in their school career. We need to tell them of the Open Learning opportunities that will face them in further education, in higher education and in training for industry, commerce and the professions. We need to tell them that many failures in higher education are caused by the students' failure to organise themselves as learners. Secondary education is *a preparation for adult life*.

3. It helps students to learn how to learn. They acquire the skills of the good student but also develop their own approaches and strategies to learning and become capable of applying these new insights in all their new learning tasks. We can't *teach* them how to learn in a theoretical way and hope that they will be able to apply the ideas in all their work. *Skills* aren't acquired that way. Would you teach a boy how to swim by sending him on a course of lectures? Far better to let him first get into the water and get the *feel* of it. It is all about trial and error, and practice, and building up experience and confidence, and being supported and encouraged. When, but only when, all that has been done, then there is a place for some instruction *as and when it is needed*. A useful definition of a skill is that it is

11

the ability to perform to a high standard, without *necessarily* being able to explain the rules that govern the performance.

4.   It helps students to get the benefits of differentiation. They are all different and we need to adjust to the needs, abilities and interests of the individual.

These are ambitious aims and they are easier to state than to achieve. Nevertheless they can be achieved if careful attention is given to techniques and styles.

But you may also think that being more student-centred will help the school to function more efficiently. There are enough problems and pressures around and teachers are constantly seeking solutions. It may be worthwhile to take a quick look at *necessity*.

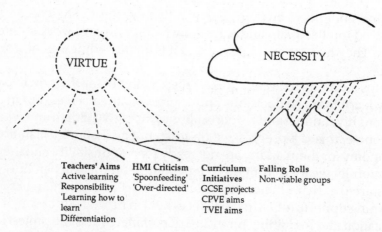

Teachers' Aims	HMI Criticism	Curriculum	Falling Rolls
Active learning	'Spoonfeeding'	Initiatives	Non-viable groups
Responsibility	'Over-directed'	GCSE projects	
'Learning how to		CPVE aims	
learn'		TVEI aims	
Differentiation			

Supported Self-Study — sources of inspiration and pressure

NECESSITY

You might think that when your students are capable of working more independently of their teachers there might be some saving in teachers' time.

We need to be careful in our thinking about this. The amount of saved time is likely to be small; but the number of possible uses of that time is endless! So while it may be helpful to list some of the possible uses, we must constantly remind ourselves that schools will have to be very selective. There is no chance that Supported Self-Study will make much more than a small dent in the side of these problems.

There is another danger. It would be wrong to introduce Supported Self-Study solely on the grounds of necessity. If it were done badly, without sufficient regard to the virtues described above, it could not be justified.

Here are some of the uses to which the saved time might be put.

More time allocated to teachers for 'development' purposes

In an ideal world this would be the main use of saved time. 'Better Schools' (DES 1985) made a case for school management to try to create more time for planning, preparation, assessment work, course development and staff development. With all the increased demands on schools, this need has become desperate.

Minority subjects preserved through reduced contact time

For a variety of reasons, where students are given options some groups may be thought to be 'not viable'. It does seem a nonsense to allocate exactly the same amount of time to a class of four as to a class of twenty-four. Of course, it is not a simple arithmetical relationship (24 students require 6 periods, therefore 4 students require 1 period!). There are fixed demands on a teacher's time regardless of the size of the group. But there are the variables (especially marking and monitoring) which make a case for some reduction in contact time.

A better way of managing heterogeneous groups

There is not likely to be any saving of time here but, where a group of students is very mixed, by virtue of ability or previous experience or examination objectives, Supported Self-Study provides a system for effective management.

Demands for continuous assessment of course work

These demands are now common. Supported Self-Study provides a systematic way of managing. Some teacher time may be saved where students are given time to get on with their project work but this is bound to be swallowed up because of the increased work-load that this arrangement imposes on the teacher.

Individual and minority group needs

These are too numerous to mention but, when Supported Self-Study gets on the agenda of a school, it will be called on whenever individual or small group needs emerge. The response is often very desirable from the students' point of view but the net effect for the teacher is more likely to be an increase in time demands, not a reduction.

So schools are right when they concentrate on the *virtue* of Supported Self-Study and regard the savings in teacher time as a small occasional bonus.

So what is Supported Self-Study?

It is nothing new. The basic ideas have been around for a long time. But the record of achievement of student-centred systems is not good. There have been mistakes and SSS is not repeating them. So, for a start, here are a few things that SSS is *not*.

1. *It is NOT a do-it-yourself system of education.* It is not inviting school students to manage without a teacher; it is not distance learning; and it is not even Open Learning (although it is certainly more open than the worst kinds of class teaching). Students in secondary schools are not ready for total independence; but they do need to be helped to grow towards it. So the teacher is more important than ever.

2. *It is NOT a laissez-faire system of education.* It is not an invitation to them to do it their own way — how they like, when they like, where they like, if they like! It should be thought of as a training in self-discipline. The skilful teacher allows discretion and decision-making according to the capability of each learner.

3. *It is NOT a demand that students should always work on their own.* There is little value in always working alone. Young learners, more than most, need the companionship and stimulus of their fellows. But equally they do need to be able to work on their own for *some* of the time.

4. *It is NOT a system based on an endless diet of worksheets.* Nor is it a resurrection of programmed learning. It aims to develop the learner's skills in using a wide range of different resources for learning.

5. *It is NOT a monolithic system of education.* It is not to be regarded as a substitute for class teaching. It represents an attitude to learning which, while putting emphasis on the personal development of the learner, embraces a wide range of methods. Young people need variety, not monotony.

So what *is* Supported Self-Study?

There are two key concepts — *'SUPPORT'* and *'SELF'*.

If young people are to be helped *progressively* to achieve the aims of SSS, they need *support*. The amount of support needed differs according to a large number of variables — age, experience, intelligence, personal attitudes and motivation, and a lot more besides. But the kinds of support are common to all:

— the support of careful and sensitive tutoring;

— the support of good management at all levels within the school;

— the support of specially chosen learning resources.

It is the concept of support that distinguishes SSS from many of the systems of independent learning of the past. In many of these, there was too much faith in the instant autonomy of the students and in the power of specially created learning resources.

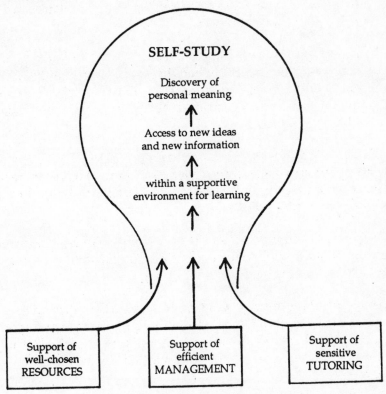

SELF-STUDY

Discovery of
personal meaning

↑

Access to new ideas
and new information

↑

within a supportive
environment for learning

↑

| Support of well-chosen RESOURCES | Support of efficient MANAGEMENT | Support of sensitive TUTORING |

The concept of Supported Self-Study

The concept of 'self' is important. Learning is an intensely personal experience. It is tied in closely with a person's total development as a human being. No amount of energetic teaching or clear exposition can overcome the simple fact that a person acquires new knowledge and understanding only in so far as he or she is able to make it personal and to own it. Most efforts in education are concentrated on presentation and delivery of knowledge and ideas, when they should be giving much greater attention to creating the right environment for learning and helping the learner to learn. Instead of tinkering with courses — adding a course here, taking away a course there, endlessly revising the curriculum, we should start recognising that meaning does not belong to the knowledge that we present but resides in the experience of the learner. Learning, like communication, is the act of the receiver! So finding ways of helping young people to *discover personal meaning* for themselves is the guiding principle in SSS.

Where in the school should Supported Self-Study be found?

Everywhere! In the secondary school it should start in the lower school by building on the styles of the good primary school. It is wrong that the student-led style of the good primary school should be ignored when the students arrive in the secondary school. Of course there are differences; in the secondary school the work cannot be 100% child-led. But this is a *progressive* training towards greater responsibility and every small step in the right direction counts. A useful start is to observe the organisation of classroom work in the upper classes of neighbouring primary schools; and then a smooth transition can be organised.

Further up the school, especially where the students have received some early training, the arrangements can become more flexible and make bigger demands on the students' responsibility. There are no hard and fast rules about supervision and support during self-study. As in the lower school, much can be accomplished by allowing time for self-study during the normal class lessons. Schools can also organise self-study time in libraries and private study areas with supervision and general counselling support. This kind of support is not likely to be subject specialist support but more concerned with general organisation, study skills, learning strategies and coping skills. Its value to individual students can be of dramatic significance — an invaluable extra support for the subject specialist.

Finally, many older students can have time allocated to a subject which is 'non-contact' time, in which there is no direct supervision or support during the self-study period itself. It should be the aim to let every student ultimately have the experience of self-study of this kind; it is part of the growing up process.

So, throughout the school, SSS should be an integral part of the normal subject teaching arrangements.

But SSS can and should appear off the timetable and outside the normal class grouping. The possibilities for greater flexibility in the working life of the school are enormous. At its most ambitious, this might represent a fundamental restructuring of the working day, the school week and the school year. At its most simple level, greater flexibility can be achieved by creating some self-study opportunities for all students. How all these arrangements might be organised, supervised and tutored is an important topic for discussion in a later section.

SSSIT—B

Supported Self-Study for whom?

By now the answer should be obvious. For all of them! And right across the curriculum. Every subject department should aim to offer some SSS experiences to its students. Here are some approaches.

1. Choose certain topics which lend themselves well to this kind of approach and prepare for them on SSS lines — *in series*.

2. Use the SSS approach *in parallel* with other styles for certain aspects of the syllabus. For example, a science department may do some class teaching for the theoretical input, organise its laboratory work in a traditional way and give some time to 'investigations' which are organised and tutored on SSS lines.

3. Use the SSS approach as a better way of organising and monitoring homework. This might involve one period of class time and the homework time being treated as self-study time, with tutoring taking place during the class period.

SSS can help particularly with a wide variety of special needs. Here are some of them.

1. A subject group falls to a size which it is thought cannot justify a full allocation of staff time. Using slightly reduced contact time and SSS methods, the group is able to survive. This arrangement needs to be introduced with sensitivity by senior management. It should be obvious that because a teacher can help in the survival of a minority subject through SSS, it does not follow that the idea can be extended indefinitely so that the teacher is asked to take on a much larger work-load.

2. Problems of timetable prevent some students from joining a chosen group. This is a common problem with 16+ resits but it often occurs within option arrangements in the upper part of the school.

3. The school is concerned about its exceptionally able students. Can they be given additional stimulus and challenge without permanently segregating them from their fellows?

4. There is a demand for short support courses. For example, a number of

A-level courses require maths support — biology, geography, economics, sociology, as well as the physical sciences. Other examples are study skills, English skills and information skills.

5. There is a demand for short enrichment courses: electronics, computer programming, media studies.

6. The school wishes to give additional support to minority groups. For example, a school might wish to give additional support to its ethnic minority groups. Occasional well-conducted tutorials in small groups are likely to give great help in overcoming technical problems with language and also enhance the self-confidence of the group within the community.

7. Students who are at home for long periods, or in hospital, may request that they should be given work and have it supervised. If good self-study materials are available and the subject specialist is willing to co-operate, the teaching staff at the hospital may feel able to give valuable help.

8. New arrivals in the school may find problems in matching the new curriculum options with the old. SSS can help the transition.

9. Where students are assigned to work outside the school — community service, work experience, courses at FE colleges or other schools — SSS can help to provide a disciplined framework and a regular link back to the school.

10. Some students may find the school's normal examination load more than they would wish or need and would prefer to have some consolidation time. The use of SSS in this kind of situation can be very powerful and make a big difference to the peace of mind and motivation of the students involved.

These are only examples. There are many more applications for SSS.

Where a school has SSS on its 'agenda', then whenever individual problems arise, the possibilities of an SSS solution are examined.

So SSS is serving both in the classroom and away from the classroom; within the timetable and off the timetable. The principles are basically the same.

What does Supported Self-Study look like? Here are the basic essentials.

SSS is a two-stroke operation.

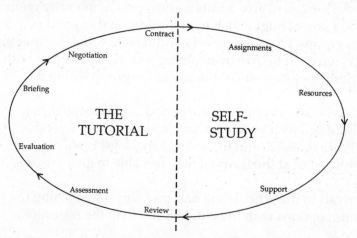

The management cycle

The students have a tutorial, which is followed by a period of self-study, which is followed by a tutorial, and so on. There seems to be nothing remarkable in that, yet it is most noticeable how many systems of independent learning work on an assumption that the teacher's role is purely reflexive. 'Get on with your work on your own. Come to me when you have problems.' This is a sure recipe for failure! Either there will be so many problems that the teacher will be submerged, or important problems will not get raised at all. Young students often have difficulty in deciding whether or not to expose their problems. The system should be designed to help them.

The tutorial is the key. Only two things have to be done at the tutorial:

1.   A thorough review and assessment of the work done during the previous self-study phase.

2.   A thorough briefing for the work that is to be done during the next self-study phase.

Only two things but their importance cannot be underestimated. Your main task in developing work in SSS is to get these two tasks done to a high standard.

It is at the tutorial that the work-plan for the self-study phase is made. In the early stage of SSS, students need to be firmly guided as to what they should do, how they should do it, how their time should be allocated, and so on. As they grow in experience, more discretion should be allowed to them and bigger demands made on them. When that stage is reached, the organising teacher will need to give attention to the additional support facilities that the school and/or the community can offer — libraries, workshops, study areas, computer facilities, other supporting tutors and mentors. But at the beginning the tutorial is all important.

Length of tutorials and the frequency of tutorials are matters which depend on the age and experience of the students. These will be discussed later within some specific contexts.

However, the optimum size of the tutorial group seems to be the same regardless of the age and experience of the students. It is five. In some situations the number has to be allowed to grow to eight but life begins to get difficult at that level. Throughout, the style of the tutorial is participatory; the tutor's skills are different from the skills of classroom teaching. There is much to be said on this later.

So far we have made no reference to resources, one of the main components of an SSS system. The reason is that it is perfectly possible to run a successful SSS programme without buying or creating additional resources. And it is equally possible to run a disastrous programme using a very rich supply of varied resources. Resources are not the keystone of an SSS system; the keystone is the tutoring and the way in which the whole thing is managed. However, this is not to say that a *well-conducted* SSS programme wouldn't benefit from a massive injection of good and varied resources. This will be explored thoroughly in a later section.

At this stage in the description of the basic model, the practical teacher will be saying 'It would be lovely to spend all my time tutoring small groups. But I don't have classes of five students!' This brings us to the very heart of SSS — the problems and the opportunities.

This needs to be said very firmly. *THE SMALL-GROUP TUTORIAL IS SO POWERFUL AND SO EFFECTIVE AS A LEARNING EXPERIENCE THAT NO EFFORT SHOULD BE SPARED TO ACHIEVE IT AS A REGULAR FEATURE OF THE STUDENTS' SCHOOL EXPERIENCE.* The basic argument of this guide is that it can be done. So we now need to get down to practical matters.

Part 2

GETTING STARTED IN SUPPORTED SELF-STUDY

Setting up a small-scale trial

Small is beautiful!

The best way to get started is to set up a small-scale trial. This means that you can try out Supported Self-Study while keeping complications down to a minimum and you can easily correct any mistakes. More important, it gives you some experience to build on. You find out easily what works well in your situation with your students and you can build on that.

So what constitutes a small-scale trial?

Concentrate the trial on one or two classes, no more. Choose classes where the prospects of success are good. This means go for the class which is small in numbers and which contains a good number of well-motivated students with a high degree of self-confidence. There is no virtue at all in adopting a 'test to destruction' attitude. We can work our way round to the more difficult situations when we have acquired a little experience.

Limit the trial to one unit of work with a lifetime of no more than a few weeks. This means that you can give a little extra effort in preparation. But an even more valuable advantage is that you can take time at the end to reflect on the experience and to come to conclusions about how to progress further. There is nothing worse with a new system than the feeling of having stepped on to a treadmill which you have to keep going at all costs.

Choose a unit of work which lends itself well to the SSS approach. We have already said that SSS is not a stand alone system. It is best used as part of a broad repertoire of teaching and learning strategies. Some topics are best approached through class teaching; others undoubtedly benefit from the SSS style. The choice for your trial is important. Although you might eventually hope to use the SSS style for investigative work involving individual or small group presentations, this might be rather ambitious for the first trial, especially if your students are new to this kind of work. It might be better to try them out on a simple 'development' job where the introductory work has already been done through class teaching. This is very much like the style of many good teachers — class work to start the topic off, followed by some individual work to carry it forward.

Involving other people

Of course, it is useful to seek the acceptance and moral support of senior management and they will no doubt appreciate the promise of a brief report at the end. But before you get down to the actual preparations, think about actively involving other people in your trial. Don't overdo this; too many advisers and supporters can be counterproductive but you should have on your side at least one sympathetic colleague and the students themselves. Your colleague will serve as a useful sounding board and could even help in a systematic way, as we shall explain later. Your students do really need to feel that they are part of an interesting trial which could be a great benefit to them. So it needs to be explained. Explain the reasons for working in these ways.

★ They will meet more 'open learning' opportunities in further and higher education and in training for industry, commerce and the professions.

★ In the future, adult learners will be expected to be much more autonomous. This is helping them to acquire the necessary techniques and disciplines.

★ They must not think that they are going to be abandoned by their teacher and left to flounder on their own. On the contrary, this will be a disciplined way of working. They will have greater expectations put on them and they will be held answerable. Monitoring of their work is likely to be more intensive.

★ However, they will get the benefits of much more intensive and individual support through group tutoring.

★ In no sense will this be a 'sloppy' approach to learning.

Explanations like this are designed to give a clear image of the two key concepts — *support* and *discipline*.

Then it is important to enlist their support as participants in the trial. Explain that you don't expect to get it perfect first time and that their observations and suggestions will be helpful and valuable. Explain the outline of the ways of working and allow them to ask questions about it. Give them some idea of the kind of questions you might be asking them later on.

The outline might sound something like the following.

1. We shall introduce the topic in the normal way through class teaching and this will be followed by some individual tasks — nothing new in that.

2. Then we shall go into SSS mode. For this you will be assigned to tutorial groups. Each group will have frequent short tutorials. At each tutorial, the group will review and assess the work that has already been done and then go on to examine the next set of tasks to be attempted. At the end of each tutorial, each member of the group will have a clear contract setting out the details of the work to be attempted and describing exactly what kind of end-product will be required.

3. We shall eventually return to the class teaching mode. This will give us an opportunity to summarise and revise, and also to reflect on the SSS experience.

These are the kind of questions that I shall probably ask you at the end of the trial.

1. During the periods of self-study, did you always feel quite clear about what was expected of you, how much discretion you had in the performance of the tasks, what resources were available to you and what the finished product should look like? Where uncertainty existed, can you make suggestions about how that might have been prevented.

2. How much value did you place on the tutorials? Were they stimulating? Did you feel that you got enough opportunity to take an active part? Do you think they were sufficiently businesslike, getting on with the job rather than indulging in rambling discussion? Did they represent a good use of time? What suggestions have you for improving the effect of the tutorials?

3. What were your general impressions? Is it a more effective way of learning? Do you feel any benefits by being asked to take on more responsibility? What overall changes could you suggest which might bring about improvements?

With these basic decisions made about the setting up of a small-scale trial, we are now ready to start the actual preparation.

Preparing the small-scale trial

Planning

Planning a unit of work involves thinking about four essentials.

1. The target group. Who are they? What are their needs? What are their special characteristics?

2. The educational objectives appropriate for this unit of work. What capabilities and skills do we wish to develop? What new knowledge and understanding do we wish them to acquire?

3. The content area covered by the unit.

4. The arrangements to evaluate the contribution that this unit of work has made to the whole course?

Now this kind of planning is not unique to SSS. It is the stock in trade of every good teacher, regardless of the methods to be used, so it is not proposed to discuss them in detail. It is assumed that the unit of work has been used before and much of the planning thinking has already been done. It is particularly important, however, that there is a clear understanding about the educational objectives of the unit. This helps to focus one's mind during the tutorial sessions.

Resources preparation

The immediate instinct is to think that introducing SSS means having specially designed resources. This used to be true in the past much more than in the present. Formerly, school textbooks were formidable objects, verbose and monotonous in their design and making little concession to the learner struggling with new knowledge and ideas. Today, textbooks are much better and the good ones make excellent self-study texts — *when they are properly supported.*

Certainly you should aim to conduct your small-scale trial as far as possible using *the resources that you already have available.* If you feel that the resources are not suitable, it would be better to choose a different unit for the trial rather than to undertake the enormous task of seeking or creating alternative resources.

Let us think of resources under three main headings:

1. The course book. This is the textbook or resource which provides the comprehensive but concise statement of the main outlines of the unit of work. It gives the student the structure of the new knowledge and is invaluable for revision.

2. The enrichment resources. These are all other materials which might be used to enliven and enrich the work. Some of these will be held within the subject department; others will be available elsewhere, particularly in or via the school library. For a well resourced unit, these resources would be in a wide range of media.

3. The assignments. When students are using a very wide range of resources, they can often benefit from additional guidance in the form of assignments prepared by their own teacher. These do not attempt to provide the substance of the new knowledge; instead they offer guidance on what resources to use, how to set about the tasks, how to present the finished product and what are the important issues and likely problems associated with this work. Often, but not necessarily always, they are produced by the teacher.

SSS schemes vary in the emphasis they place on each of these three types of resource. Some rely only on a single course book; some do not use a course book at all, emphasising the wide range of resources and the support of carefully produced assignments; others use a course book with a set of assignments to help the student use the course book for a particular purpose. For the purposes of a small-scale trial, it is wise to keep things as simple as possible. Ultimately, we want to use SSS as a strategy for exploiting a rich resource base but the first need is to get the system operating smoothly.

So you might settle for your existing course book and a small collection of enrichment resources. You could probably manage without making any assignments but, if you feel this is essential, you should consult the Reference Section to help you to do this. Remember, though, that the tutorial will be your main opportunity for giving guidance; and this is far more powerful than even the most carefully produced assignments.

Preparations for self-study

Where and when will your students carry out their self-study work?

If your trial is with a large lower school class, then your scope is somewhat limited. They will almost certainly do most of it in the classroom under your supervision at the times allocated on the timetable. The only possible extensions of this are:

1. It may be possible to release individuals or small groups to do specific work at other locations on the site (particularly the school library) where the school policy and arrangements allow this.

2. Homework. SSS is a particularly lively way of making really good use of this time.

If your trial is with a smaller class of older pupils, the range of possibilities is much greater. They may well be on a programme which assumes a certain amount of off-site work and they may have allocated time for self-study with non-specialist supervision or with no supervision. The chief need is for clarity. Whatever the arrangements, everyone concerned (senior management, colleagues, students) must know and have agreed the conditions. Generally speaking, it is wise to err on the side of caution. If the students are inexperienced, some monitoring or supervision is advisable.

Next, arrangements will need to be made to give the students access to the resources they will need during their self-study sessions. This may involve negotiation with other teachers, librarians, technicians and senior management. Again, it is impossible to give universal prescriptions; we can only emphasise the need for knowledge and understanding of all concerned.

Preparations for tutorials

The first task is to establish the tutorial groups.

How many in a group? The optimum is probably five. Fewer tends to produce insufficient stimulus; more tends to allow one or two to play passive roles (eight should be regarded as the absolute maximum).

How many such groups can the teacher handle? It gets difficult above four — so much so that it is probably wise to regard this as the more important of the two limiting factors. Where a choice seems possible between reducing the number of groups and reducing group size, prefer the former.

So, in practice, it would work out like this:

Class of 12 students = 2 groups of 6 students (*the alternative would be 3 groups of 4; but 6 is probably a better group size than 4 and 2 groups are easier to manage than 3*)

Class of 20 students = 4 groups of 5 students (*3 groups of 7+7+6 also worth considering*)

Class of 28 students = 4 groups of 7 students

Class of 30 students = 4 groups of 7+7+8+8 (*must not exceed 4 groups*)

The next problem is to establish the composition of the groups. What are the criteria to be used in allocating individual students to the groups?

It does not seem possible to suggest a 'best buy' here. In other words, whatever criteria you have adopted, the methods of SSS can be made to yield valuable results. So it is simply a question of referring to your own subject and situation, the policy of your school and your own preferences and convictions. Only a few general points need to be made.

★ Avoid having a tutorial group entirely composed of slow or reluctant learners; it will be an uphill task.

★ Normally try to keep a balance between the sexes; the different styles can be mutually supportive. On the other hand, you may have a definite educational reason for wanting segregation. At least be clear about the reasons for your decision.

★ Even after determining your main criteria, you may find you have a little scope for manipulating the composition of the groups. Do it positively to try to ensure that each group has a good balance of styles and interests.

What is the frequency and duration of the tutorials? The two are clearly related. There is no absolute answer. For a first trial and always with inexperienced students or with larger classes, it is best to go for high frequency and short tutorials. This is not SSS at its highest peak of achievement but it is a start in the right direction. The teacher in control of a large class will need to divide time between intensive tutorials and more general support and supervision. Take, for example, our class of 28 organised in 4 groups of 7 students. Suppose that the weekly allocation is 10% (about 150 minutes), timetabled in three sessions. It would be sufficient to aim at the start for each group to have two 10-minute tutorials each week. This would use up 80 minutes in tutorials, leaving the teacher with 70 minutes for general support and supervision.

Introduction through class teaching

There is a lot to be said for using class teaching for the introduction of a new unit of work.

★ It provides an 'advance organiser' for all the students, which helps them to see the structure of the new knowledge and understanding and how it fits with previous knowledge and experience. It is like offering them a map and a guidebook *before* they start on a journey.

★ It can be an inspiring and motivating experience, with the teacher using methods and media which will appeal both intellectually and emotionally. The experiences of people can often be valuable in this work, whether through written accounts or the teacher's own vivid description.

★ It ensures that the whole class has a common starting point and has a shared understanding of what the unit is about and what the main objectives are.

There is no need to detail all the techniques of good whole class presentation. Clearly, we are not talking about delivering a lecture but rather providing an experience which involves the students as much as is possible in this large group situation.

Making the transition to Supported Self-Study

A little practical difficulty now presents itself. How do we make the shift from the class teaching mode into the SSS mode? This could be the cause of some untidiness which would get us off to a bad start. There needs to be some kind of bridging activity.

Probably the simplest way is to regard the first self-study task as a task common to all. The briefing for it should be a whole class exercise. The task could be a simple one to be done individually and a natural outcome of the class teaching which has just preceded it.

The common task should be long enough in duration to allow the teacher to conduct very short tutorials with each tutorial group in turn. This will be looking ahead to the second task which the group will undertake. This has the effect of a starter motor, getting the engine into its cycle of operation.

Some management aspects of the SSS cycle

Getting the cycle started is not the only problem. There are a number of issues which need to be resolved.

1. *Should all the groups be working on the same tasks?* They can do this provided sufficient resources are available. An alternative is to operate a 'circus', the four groups rotating through four different tasks. This is economical in the use of resources (as many science teachers and English teachers will testify). In some subjects, the circus does not seem right because of the sequential nature of the subject matter; but close examination often shows that it can be used successfully. For example, in history, for any given period of time there may be four parallel topics that need examination; and they can probably be studied in any order. It is also worth observing that the logical sequences that we have in our minds are not always necessary for learners who are new to a topic.

2. *Should all the pupils in a tutorial group be given exactly the same tasks?* They could be but in practice it is likely that the teacher will suggest, during tutorials, different tasks which are adapted to individual needs and abilities.

3. *Is it really possible to individualise in the way just described when tutoring a group of seven students?* A lot can be accomplished. You can spend some of the time relating to the group as a whole but you should aim the briefing for new tasks at individuals, using the other members of the group to help with suggestions. Of course it is a compromise. But the alternative of trying to tutor each individual in turn puts too much time pressure on the teacher and too much psychological pressure on the student.

4. *Should the tutorials for a group take place at the same time each week?* No, it is better to arrange each tutorial when the group is ready for it.

5. *So what about slow workers and fast workers?* The members of a group are bound to finish a given task at different times. How do we cope with this? First, try to make some adjustments during the briefing stage of the tutorial. For a slow student, you need to decide whether to insist on a brisker pace of working or whether to accept that the student is working to capacity and needs help to decide priorities so that a balanced product can be delivered. For a fast student, you need to decide whether to insist

on a more thorough and painstaking effort (not slapdash) or whether to encourage the student to take on additional assignments. For this latter purpose, it is essential to have a number of interesting and worthwhile additional assignments which any student can turn to if faced with a period of waiting before the tutorial. It is unwise in Supported Self-Study to allow, or encourage, unrestricted self-pacing. The consequences are somewhat damaging: students finish up working in isolation from each other and the teacher suffers from mental exhaustion trying to keep in touch with so many different work programmes.

6. *What happens in all this to the very slow and the very insecure?* The answer is to bend the system a little in their favour. One of their big needs is more frequent reference to the teacher. They can be encouraged to do this in addition to their attendance at tutorials. They do not need additional tutorials, just more frequent check-ups.

7. *How is it possible with a large class to guarantee that those on self-study are working when the teacher is occupied in tutorial?* To a certain extent this is a chicken and egg situation. This can be tricky at first. There are a number of factors which will contribute to success.

    a) A good tutorial with clear briefing and high expectations clearly expressed.

    b) The use of resources which have been carefully selected for self-study so that problems are kept to a minimum.

    c) The frequent tour of the class to make sure that everyone is on task and to help with difficulties and to give encouragement where needed.

The general principle in the management of Supported Self-Study is to have a clear and firm framework of procedures but to be ready to adjust and adapt in the light of situations and individual needs. At the end of the day, Supported Self-Study is an art rather than a mechanical system. Nevertheless, it does help to start in a fairly systematic way.

The conduct of the tutorial

This is a question of style. There is no universal truth about this. Think of the gap that needs to be bridged. On one side is the ultimate goal of SSS — the truly autonomous learner. On the other side are your students as they are now. If you feel that your students are a long way from the ultimate goal, then they need firm support and guidance. This probably means that, at first, you have to be somewhat prescriptive. The first lesson for them to learn is how to deliver work in the agreed manner, to acceptable standards and at the agreed time. When they report regularly in small groups, they are much more likely to develop good habits.

But the mark of a good tutor is that there is a constant drive towards greater responsibility of the students and their more active involvement in the whole learning process. Supported Self-Study is a *training*.

The tasks of the tutorial

The tutorial needs to be conducted in four domains.

1. The Intellectual. The students need to be helped to adopt an intellectual approach to their work and to be conscious of their own thought processes.

2. The Affective. Each student needs to feel valued and respected as a person and that the tutorial is supportive in a personal way.

3. The Social. The students need to experience the stimulation of helping and challenging each other and to feel that the group is an aid to learning and progress.

4. The Managerial. The students need to understand the need for efficient and disciplined ways of working, both at the tutorial and during the self-study phases.

The agenda of the tutorial

A typical tutorial which takes place at the end of one set of tasks and before the beginning of another would have the following agenda items.

1. Review of the work just done. Factual and reflective.

2. Assessment of the same work. This might be done by the teacher at first but sooner or later it is good to involve the students themselves.

3. Briefing for the new tasks to be undertaken.

4. Negotiation about resources, deadlines, standards, priorities, etc.

5. Contract for each student. At its simplest, this could be the student's notes made during the tutorial, signed by both student and teacher.

Evaluating the small-scale trial

This should not be an elaborate or formal affair. In practice, you will find during the trial that so many issues are raised and so many fresh decisions are made that the thing will evaluate itself!

However, there is a lot to be said for keeping systematic notes of problems and reminders for the future.

Make use of your support colleague. Even just talking through the experiences will be valuable but if some opportunity has occurred for your colleague to witness any of the tutorials or talk to the students during periods of self-study, some very valuable insights may have been gained.

Likewise, make use of your students. Give them a simple questionnaire, worded suitably for their age. Use their responses to make an agenda for a class discussion on the trial. They can be so helpful and rarely attempt to take advantage of the privilege.

Finally, use the results of your reflections to guide your thinking about the future. Do you need further limited trials or can you begin to expand the use of SSS into new areas?

You will almost certainly by now have a long list of things that you would like to do and things that you would like the school to do. One thing is certain: you will have to be selective and make a list of priorities. It is intended that the Reference Section of this book should help you.

The description in this section has assumed a large class confined to one classroom. This is probably the most difficult situation to manage and most teachers would wish to break free, at least partly, from some of these constraints. It is hoped that study of the Reference Section will help readers to see how the basic principles described so far can be applied in much more flexible and open situations.

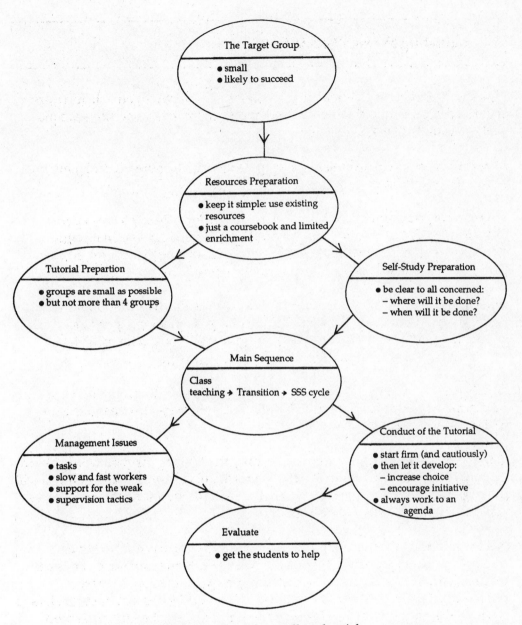

The Target Group

- small
- likely to succeed

Resources Preparation

- keep it simple: use existing resources
- just a coursebook and limited enrichment

Tutorial Preparation

- groups are small as possible
- but not more than 4 groups

Self-Study Preparation

- be clear to all concerned:
  – where will it be done?
  – when will it be done?

Main Sequence

Class teaching → Transition → SSS cycle

Management Issues

- tasks
- slow and fast workers
- support for the weak
- supervision tactics

Conduct of the Tutorial

- start firm (and cautiously)
- then let it develop:
  – increase choice
  – encourage initiative
- always work to an agenda

Evaluate

- get the students to help

The essentials of a small-scale trial

Part 3

REFERENCE SECTION

An introduction to tutoring

High quality tutoring is the best support that the teacher can give to students who are being trained in Supported Self-Study. When it is done well, it achieves things that are rarely possible in class teaching.

Good teachers can become good tutors but a word of warning is necessary. It is not just a matter of believing in the aims of SSS; one has to make *conscious* adjustments to style and techniques and to be humble enough to recognise that one's previous experience is not a guarantee of instant success.

The teaching profession is not unusual in this respect. The problem can be observed in countless human relations situations. It exists between superior and subordinate, between the experienced and the inexperienced, between the older and the younger, between those who work at the head office and those who work in the field, between parents and children, between management and workers, between government and people. It is natural enough to believe that one's job is to explain, to inform, to direct, to advise — in short, to *communicate* as clearly as possible. But this isn't sensitive enough to the reality of these situations. People work, or learn, or achieve things only to the extent that they *have a sense of ownership*. Putting it this way carries the argument beyond merely 'involving' them; it emphasises *their* initiative, *their* leadership, *their* decisions and *their* answerability.

So good tutoring does not come naturally to people in authority. This recognition must be the starting point for any teacher. Getting them to feel this sense of ownership is the first priority. It is not simple because the ownership has to include the ownership of the constraints, the external demands and the perceptions of other people! This is the stark reality behind 'training them to accept greater responsibility for their own learning'. It is a very ambitious aim for the teaching profession and will not yield to vague, casual or sentimental approaches.

The case for the group tutorial

The first choice is between tutoring the individual student, tutoring in small groups and tutoring the whole class.

Tutoring the individual student seems attractive at first sight because it should be possible to adjust accurately to the individual's needs and abilities. But there are weaknesses.

★ The student is under great psychological pressure in this one-to-one relationship and may fail to respond in the way that the teacher hopes.

★ The student will be deprived of the stimulus of fellow students.

★ There will be severe pressures on the teacher's time.

★ The teacher will have to conduct so many tutorials that the students will have to sustain very long periods of self-study between them. This will not work for many younger and less-experienced students.

Tutoring the whole class at once seems attractive to the teacher who is concerned about the economic use of own time. But again there are weaknesses.

★ Feedback is difficult and unreliable. How much have they been able to participate? Have they really understood what they have to do?

★ Much time has to be spent on organisation and 'business' and discipline instead of the substance of the learning.

So tutoring in small groups (of about five students) seems to be the best arrangement.

1. The group is big enough to be intellectually stimulating and socially supportive.

2. The group is small enough to enable each individual to feel important and responsible. In groups of this size it is fairly easy to ensure that no one individual gets left out or is allowed to opt out of the group's thinking and effort.

3. The teacher can concentrate the action so that a very high proportion of the time is spent on the substance of the learning ('on task').

4. The teacher can be reasonably economical in the use of his/her own time and effort.

Arrangements for tutorials

The size of the tutorial group

We have already suggested that the optimum is 5 and given reasons. The workable range is probably between 4 and 8. Less than 4 students will tempt the tutor into playing too dominant a role in order to keep things moving ahead. With 8 or more students it becomes very difficult to deal with them as individuals and there is an increasing tendency for some to withdraw from the action.

The number of tutorial groups

Teachers usually find it difficult to handle more than four such groups. This is especially so with large lower school classes where the students on self-study must remain under the supervision of the teacher. So, in this situation, there will be four groups of 7 or 8 students in each group. This is not the easiest of arrangements for SSS but it can operate well with clear and firm, but short, tutorials and careful attention to monitoring procedures.

The composition of tutorial groups

On what basis should students be allocated to tutorial groups? By academic ability? By friendship? By teacher decision to achieve a 'balanced mix'? SSS doesn't seem to *demand* any of these. It can bring about improvements in the quality of learning in any group, however composed. So the message is simply to arrange the groups' composition according to your own convictions or the policy of the school. And remember that it is what happens during the tutorial that really makes the difference.

The frequency and length of tutorials

These two variables depend on the age, experience and capabilities of the students involved. At one extreme is project work in the 5th and 6th forms and the 'resit' of 16+ exams for sixth-formers. For these, one intensive tutorial per week can be enough. At the other extreme is the large lower school class where very short tutorials take place very frequently. Here, in a one-hour lesson devoted largely to self-study assignments, the teacher might give each of four tutorial groups a short tutorial of about 5 to 10 minutes. This would leave plenty of time between the tutorials for general supervision and support. Of course, this is not tutoring at its most sophisticated. It is, however, an important step down the road. The first need of the younger students is to learn the discipline of working independently for a short period of time, guided by a simple assignment and delivering the finished product on time. Let them learn to walk before we ask them to run.

The objectives of the tutorial

The objectives are in four domains: intellectual, affective, social and managerial.

Intellectual

'Learning how to learn' is a broad aim for SSS. It approaches this, not through 'lessons' on how to learn but through experience and practice. It is concerned with the *application* of study skills in real learning situations. But a good tutorial goes beyond the individual skills into the strategic approach to studying. Students are encouraged to think about their own thought processes and to become more analytical. They learn how to combine the individual skills into longer term strategies in order to achieve their goals. They learn the benefits of flexibility in thinking and the use of imagination.

Affective

Good tutoring is supportive in a personal sense. It helps students to organise themselves and to get the best out of their school work. It helps them to see the relevance and the meaning for them. It helps them to integrate their school work with their lives outside the school. It recognises that learning is an intensely *personal* thing.

Social

The tutorial contributes to the social development of the students. They get the benefits of sharing, mutually supporting, collaborating and competing. These are in their own right but they also enhance the quality of the learning itself.

Managerial

The tutorial is an experience of firm intention, of discipline and of a systematic approach to getting things done. It has the 'bias towards action' which is a hallmark of success in all walks of life. The good tutorial is like a well-conducted business meeting.

ALL OF WHICH ADDS UP TO A VERY ADULT WAY OF LEARNING!

Check-lists for a tutorial

The potential of a good tutorial is one of the most exciting aspects of Supported Self-Study but achieving the good tutorial is not as easy as it seems. It can be done, provided the task is approached with determination. These are the steps which might be taken at departmental level in order to achieve good tutorial styles.

1.	Get tutorial styles and objectives on the departmental agenda. Share ideas, discuss objectives and keep bringing up the subject for re-examination.

2.	Create a departmental *Policy for Tutoring*. This is a statement of the styles and techniques that the department's members are striving to achieve. It needs to be a document which is the result of discussion and the sharing of ideas. It needs to be regularly updated and used as an agenda for evaluation discussions and as a check-list for mutual observation.

3.	Encourage mutual observation, especially with specific improvements in mind. Regard the observer as the *servant* of the tutor, not as the judge. The use of the Policy for Tutoring will give a sharp focus to this. It is better to use observation to try to improve on specific aspects of the tutorial rather than to be satisfied with general overall impressions.

4.	Arrange a systematic evaluation of the department's tutoring. Get the students to contribute through the use of simple questionnaires and structured discussions.

There follows a model of a check-list for a tutorial. This is the form in which a department's Policy for Tutoring could be presented. Under the four main headings are a number of assertions which the department may have decided are the observable features of a successful tutorial. This document could be used as follows:

1.	On in-service training days as a check-list for the study of a tutorial recorded on video.

2.	As a tool to assist in a programme of mutual observation and support within a department.

3.	As a discussion document to provide an agenda for the discussion of training and development needs in the promotion of SSS.

When in use, each assertion in the document can be tested simply YES or NO, or you could use a simple rating system (say 1 to 5). The use of the document is the first step. It is used to *start* a discussion not to be the end of it!

THE GREAT DANGER FOR THE TUTORIAL IS THAT THERE MIGHT BE A GAP BETWEEN THE RHETORIC AND THE GOOD INTENTION ON THE ONE HAND AND THE ACTUAL PRACTICE ON THE OTHER. ONLY DETERMINED EFFORTS WILL BRIDGE THIS GAP.

TUTORIAL CHECK-LIST: THE INTELLECTUAL

1.   The tutor offers guidance about learning strategies.

2.   The tutor sets an example of intellectual integrity (admits errors, confesses lack of knowledge, etc).

3.   The tutor promotes an interest in the use of study skills and information skills.

4.   The tutor uses both the language of analytical thinking and of imaginative thinking, in order to help the students become more aware of their own thought processes.

5.   The students readily admit errors, lack of knowledge, confusion, etc. They can see the value of such admissions for the learning process.

6.   The students demonstrate a capacity for criticising ideas in a responsible and thoughtful way.

7.   The students constantly seek to structure their knowledge and understanding in meaningful ways.

8.   The students are not afraid to express value judgements and to have them discussed.

9.   The students demonstrate their willingness and ability to be mutually supportive in an intellectual way.

10. The tutorial is so organised that the students spend over 90% of the time actively engaged in learning.

A GOOD TUTORIAL IS AN INTELLECTUAL EXPERIENCE.

TUTORIAL CHECK-LIST: THE AFFECTIVE

1. The tutor shows a personal interest in individual students for their own sake, beyond the needs of the immediate learning task.

2. The tutor creates a warm and supportive climate.

3. The tutor uses the conventional adult courtesies in conversation with students.

4. The tutor makes frequent use of praise and encouragement for individual efforts.

5. The tutor frequently accepts a student's expression of feeling.

6. The students demonstrate a concern for the success and satisfaction of other members of the group.

7. The students are able to disagree with each other and with the teacher in a mature and non-threatening manner.

8. The students and their teacher occasionally share a sense of humour.

THE GOOD TUTORIAL ENHANCES THE SELF-RESPECT OF THE STUDENT AND ENCOURAGES THE GROWTH TOWARDS MATURITY.

TUTORIAL CHECK-LIST: THE SOCIAL

1. The action is shared fairly evenly among the members of the group.

2. The tutor promotes co-operation within the group.

3. The tutor provides opportunities for useful competition.

4. The tutor provides opportunities for the sharing of learning experiences.

5. The tutor is frequently able to play the role of observer because the students are so active, supporting and challenging each other.

6. The style of the tutorial is participatory.

7. The students show evidence of developing attention and respect for the views and actions of others.

THE GOOD TUTORIAL IS ALSO A BENEFICIAL SOCIAL EXPERIENCE.

TUTORIAL CHECK-LIST: THE MANAGERIAL

1.   The tutor demonstrates high expectations of the students.

2.   The tutorial has the air of a well-conducted business meeting.

3.   There is frequent reference to the main objectives of the work.

4.   There is frequent discussion of standards of work.

5.   The practical administrative matters are dealt with clearly and briskly.

6.   Time is devoted at the end of the tutorial to summarise and reinforce the decisions and agreements made.

7.   There is great sensitivity to the 'communications' problem. Students are regularly invited to summarise what has been stated, agreed and resolved, in order that any misconceptions are highlighted at the earliest possible moment.

8.   In pursuit of greater clarity and answerability, there is a tradition of 'getting it down in writing' — contracts.

A GOOD TUTORIAL EMPHASISES EFFICIENCY AND PARTICIPATION.

The agenda of the tutorial

If it is to be like a well-conducted business meeting, it will need to work to an agenda. The students should know the agenda (why not have a standard agenda and agree its adoption or modification at the beginning of each tutorial?). The suggestions made below are for the main headings of such an agenda.

1. *Review* the work completed during the last self-study phase. This includes factual reporting on work done, problems encountered, interesting achievements and possibilities discovered for future work.

2. Make *assessments* of the same work. Hopefully, some kind of profile records are being kept and the tutorial creates exactly the right conditions for this.

3. Give a *briefing* for the next phase of self-study. This requires clear definitions of objectives and scope of the work; identification of resources to be used; clear descriptions of tasks, problems and issues; guidance on the scope and style of the presentation.

4. Let the briefing develop as a *negotiation*. Students need to learn through experience that negotiation is an attempt to balance their own needs and interests against the perceptions of the tutor and against the demands of the external world. It is *not* an invitation to be purely self-willed.

5. Bring the tutorial to a close through the making of a *contract* with each student. This is easily done if they are encouraged to make notes during the briefing stage; the notes then can be adopted as the contract — the 'minutes of the meeting'.

AN AGENDA PROVIDES A DISCIPLINED WAY OF WORKING.

An agenda within an agenda!

Working to an agenda can certainly provide a disciplined way of working. But there is still a lot to be done if we are going to get our students to take a full and responsible part. One helpful way of approaching the agenda is to have a mini-procedure to apply to each agenda item in turn.

This order of procedure can do much to get them involved. It could look something like this:

1. This is the most important step. *Get the first thinking from one of the students* —
    the one who is most directly concerned. Let them all realise that each item
    on the agenda will *always* start with an input from one of them. They will
    come to it much more alert than if they expect to have to listen to a long
    introductory preamble. Hope for and encourage some direct student-to-
    student interaction. To help this, you should practise your non-verbal
    communication skills. If your eye is always on whoever is speaking, that
    will reinforce the feeling that it is you to whom they are speaking. Always
    ask a contributor to 'tell the group' and then look at the group, not at the
    speaker.

2. Then invite reactions from the group. Continue to encourage student-to-
    student interaction.

3. Offer your own information, ideas, suggestions and imperatives.

4. Get their reactions.

5. Summarise.

6. Get one of them to recapitulate.

As each new item on the agenda is reached, the procedure starts afresh. Of
course, in practice it will have to be much more flexible than this but having a
procedural approach like this in one's repertoire can help prevent slipping into
an over-directive style.

Getting them to participate: styles

'My students just won't contribute to serious discussion.' It is a common
enough feeling; progress can be very slow but conscious attention to *styles* and
techniques is the only way forward. Here are some 'thoughts' on style.

The Thoughts of Lao Tsu

'When the best leader's work is done,
The people say, "We did it ourselves".'

Silence is golden

Our instinct is always to intervene, to explain, to correct because we want to be
helpful. However, our very competence is the thing that inhibits them. So we
must learn to wait, learn to allow a small amount of wandering down unprofitable
paths, learn that if we wait long enough the student will make an attempt, if
only out of embarrassment!

Blessed are the meek for they shall inherit the earth

We must let them see that we don't always know, that we can get things wrong. A certain amount of fallibility keeps them alert!

Being wrong is interesting

And we must help them emulate our modest style. Don't just be considerate when they get things wrong. Use the error as the start of a profitable discussion, at the end of which the person who made the error is congratulated for starting such an interesting discussion.

Actions speak louder than words

Demonstrate a preference for getting on with things. If there is a healthy pace, students talk more freely than if a lot of time is taken up with trivialities.

Have fun

If they are enjoying it, they will contribute more. So, within reason, a little jollity will help.

Getting them to participate: techniques

Tasks that will involve them

Each student should have a small administrative duty, preferably one that demands reporting back. Work to the principle of giving a student a responsibility *just before* he/she is ready for it. Involve them also in the organisation and monitoring of the learning. Their activity here will make them better learners. Examples of this are:

★   Letting each student read and review the work of another student and letting the other student have the right of reply;

★   The 'pathfinder' technique, in which one student looks ahead at the new topic and is asked to make a specific contribution at the briefing stage (what materials are in the library, what articles in journals, where are the difficult spots, and so on);

★   Delegating parts of an overcrowded syllabus to individual students with the responsibility of providing a neat summary of the content for the use of all.

Questioning

This is a technique that really earns its keep. The main things to avoid are questions that can be answered by a 'yes' or a 'no' and questions that are too obviously tied to a sequence that is already in your mind. So good questions start with 'How . . . .' or 'Why . . . .' or 'What if . . . .' or 'What is your opinion of . . . .'

Here are some further hints:

1. Remember to *wait* for the answer!

2. Praise good answers but also preserve the self-esteem of those who give wrong answers.

3. Prompt and encourage, but unobtrusively.

4. Make sure that they are *all* involved.

5. Create a climate which delights in the bold and imaginative answer and warmly accepts the *personal* response.

6. Promote mutual respect. Condemn sarcasm and destructive criticism.

TECHNIQUES CAN SHIFT THE MOST RELUCTANT!

Getting them to participate: evaluation

Students will become much more involved in tutorials if they really believe that they can have an influence on the way that the tutorials are conducted. So involve them in the evaluation. They can be very insightful and rarely abuse the responsibility.

Start with a simple questionnaire

It need not be an elaborate thing. Just a few questions which can be the start of a discussion. However, it is good to ask them to write down their thoughts; this makes them reflect a little. Make each question specific, focusing on one aspect of the tutorial rather than being too general. Then ask for suggestions, again with each having a specific focus. For younger students, the 'sentence completion' type of question is often much enjoyed and results in some very thought-provoking answers.

Follow up with a structured discussion

Read through their answers to the questionnaire and then plan an agenda for the discussion. The aim is to get them to elaborate on and justify the points they have already made in writing. Demonstrate a willingness to listen. Beware of adopting defensive positions. The purpose of the discussion is to get them to articulate more clearly the impressions and feelings that they have about the tutorials. You don't, at the end of the day, have to be a slave to everything they say; but you are in a strong position when you have given them a lot of encouragement and help in saying it clearly.

SO TEACH THEM THE TRUE MEANING OF 'EVALUATION'.

The style of the tutorial

A good tutorial is like a well-conducted business meeting. It represents a skilful balance between two important aims.

1. To get the wholehearted involvement and co-operation of the learners. They must get a genuine sense of participation and a feeling that their knowledge is being used and their ideas and opinions respected.

2. To ensure that the work proceeds efficiently, that the syllabus is covered, that the learners don't get unnecessarily side-tracked and that standards are being set and maintained.

This is the perennial management problem. How do we balance a concern for people with a concern for performance and achievement?

In the very best tutorial, the two aims become mutually supportive. Performance is high *because* the learners are actively involved and respected; and the learners' sense of personal worth is high *because* there are high expectations of their performance.

However, this state of affairs is difficult to achieve. Constant thinking about styles can help.

Imagine that the style of an individual tutorial can be indicated by its location on a grid. The x axis represents concern for performance; the y axis represents concern for people. So the very best tutorial would score high on both axes and be placed at point A. The very worst would score low on both and be placed at point B. Most would be somewhere between these two extremes. But the really interesting point for each tutorial is the extent to which it deviates from the main diagonal which represents a balance between concern for people and a concern for performance. An excessive concern for people at the expense of performance results in a weak tutorial, devoted to comfort and sentiment. An excessive concern for performance at the expense of people results in a hard, mechanistic tutorial which does not motivate the learners.

Reflect on any tutorial that you have observed or seen on video.

1. What score would you give for 'Concern for people'?

2. What score would you give for 'Concern for performance'?

3. Compare your ratings with colleagues and try to resolve any differences.

4. Practise writing a short *constructive and helpful* report on the tutorial, indicating how the tutorial could be improved.

Other kinds of tutorials

The model described above represents the normal tutorial which takes place at the end of one self-study task and at the beginning of a new one. There can, however, be other kinds of tutorials held at different times which are simply intended to provide part of the continuous support for the learner.

Coaching sessions

These are intended to be workshops aimed at overcoming specific problems or difficulties. They may not be attended by all members of a tutorial group.

Discussions

These are intended to provide additional experience in handling the knowledge and ideas. Students should be trained to prepare for these so that they can come armed with information and argument. In this way, the experience becomes intellectually stimulating.

Personal counselling

This is intended to help an individual student resolve difficulties which may have originated outside the immediate learning situation. It is important that the subject specialist should be alert to these kinds of situations. It is not possible to separate learning from the totality of living and very often the person who can give the most effective help is the person with whom the student is in day-to-day contact.

These kinds of tutorials are clearly different from the tightly structured tutorial and their agendas need to be different, responding more to observed needs rather than to an overall design for the management of learning.

With a group of older students who have acquired some experience in SSS, it should be possible to arrange meetings at which the teacher is not present: discussions and receiving reports lend themselves well to this. When this happy state of affairs is reached, the claim about developing personal responsibility begins to take on real meaning.

The idea of negotiation

This is an essential element in the conduct of a good tutorial. The tutor wishes to involve the students, not only by getting them to be more active but also by getting them to contribute to the thinking about how the work is to be organised and presented. This is a natural implication of the participative style.

Negotiation doesn't mean letting the students decide for themselves (although there may well be many occasions when they should be allowed to do just that). Negotiation is disciplined approach to decision-making by a group of people. It is necessary when the decisions are important ones. It represents a sort of insurance policy against decisions which have not looked at all the alternatives in a thorough way.

It is a four-step process.

1. *Collect together all the facts that are likely to be relevant to the decision.* The sort of things that might be relevant in SSS are: what work has already been done; what assessment grades were given for it; what does the external syllabus demand; what opportunities or constraints might exist within the school calendar or timetable or accommodation; what support is likely to be available. This should be a shared activity in a tutorial. However, it is important that this first stage should be concerned only with *facts*, not with opinions or desires.

2. *Listen to the opinions and get the perceptions of all who are concerned with this decision.* This obviously means the students themselves and the tutor. The group should also look outside itself; it may not be practicable or desirable to get the first-hand testimony of other people but their known opinions should be 'put on the table'. Such opinions and perceptions might belong to the senior management of the school or to a chief examiner or to a local authority curriculum co-ordinator. Again, it is important to listen to all contributions and for the group to help each contributor to explain exactly

what is perceived. Criticism and debate should be withheld at this stage.

3.   *Identify the problem areas and decide what needs to be resolved.* Some real negotiation is now under way. Students should be encouraged to stay calm and not to give way to emotion. They should be encouraged to identify for themselves what the imperatives are. It is far better that this should come from them than be imposed. If the examination syllabus lays down a particular activity, there is little point in wanting not to do it!

4.   *Get an agreed statement which all have had a hand in shaping.* Students will soon learn that these agreed statements will rarely be identical with their own desires. The important thing is for them to understand the reasons behind them; and being involved in shaping the decision is far superior to any amount of careful 'explaining' after the tutor has made the decision unilaterally.

The contract

The contract is a detailed agreement setting out the decisions made during a tutorial. Its value cannot be underestimated. Young people like the adult approach, especially where they have helped in the decision-making process.

Contracts vary. Some are informal and verbal. Others are formal and written. The first runs the danger of being vague and insufficiently firm in intent. The second runs the danger of being bureaucratic and stifling of additional initiatives. There is a lot to be said for risking the second dangers in the early stages: you can always ease up in style once the routines are established — it is much more difficult to tighten up when slackness has been previously accepted.

The simplest written form of contract is to regard the notes made by the students during tutorial as the agreement. With the tutor aware that this is so, it is an easy matter when stressing important matters to pause while students make a note. The notes become a sort of 'minutes of the meeting' which can be referred to if misunderstanding arises later on.

A more formal contract can be based on a printed form. Not every section needs to be completed for each piece of work but the structure is there as a reminder.

It is then only one additional step towards integrating the work of the tutorial with the system of student records and assessments for a subject department. If the contracts are filed under students' names, then a complete record of work done and assessments is instantly available to anyone with a legitimate need to know — head of department, subject teacher and, of course, the student.

Here is a model which could easily be modified to suit the needs and styles of a subject department.

A MODEL CONTRACT

Name _____ Form _____ Date _____

Subject/Topic _____

BRIEFING

Objectives _____
_____
_____

Assignments/Resources

    Essential _____
_____

    Further suggestions _____
_____

Notes on Tasks _____
_____
_____

Notes on Presentation _____
_____

REVIEW

Student's Report _____
_____
_____

Tutor's Report _____
_____

Librarian's Report _____
_____

Assessments _____
_____

A programme for the improvement of tutoring

Tutoring is easier to talk about than to do. We have already looked at some of the problems facing anyone in a position of authority who tries, in all good faith, to make use of more participative styles. It is not that we have the wrong attitudes, wishing to keep our students in a state of permanent subjugation. It is more a question of shaking off some of the instinctive reactions of the class teacher which are often quite deeply embedded in us, even though our general philosophy is caring and student-centred.

Good teachers can become good tutors but they stand a much better chance if they are sensitive to these points.

So what needs to be done to help ourselves and our colleagues to make the shift in style towards the good tutorial which can do so much to enhance the quality of the education we offer? Here is a suggested programme for a department or for a whole school. The underlying theme is that *talking about it* has only a limited value; this is a case for *action learning* — learning through doing it.

1. *Develop a 'Policy for Tutoring' for the school or the department.* The check-lists on tutoring provided in this book would make a useful start but the aim should be to produce a distinctive and unique product which matches your own aims and styles.

2. *Use the 'Policy' as a working tool to guide all thinking and action about tutoring.* Parts of it can be used for the following purposes:

    — as an agenda for planning discussions;

    — as a tool to help in general evaluation of the work of a department;

    — as an observation schedule for use when viewing video recordings of tutorials;

    — as an observation schedule for use when a programme of mutual observation is being practised.

3. *Regularly review the 'Policy' in the light of experience.*

It must be emphasised that the programme of mutual observation is by far the most effective way of bringing about the desired changes. All the other techniques should be regarded as subordinate to it — useful in conjunction with it but never as a substitute for it.

So what do we mean by mutual observation? These are the ideal conditions:

1. A partnership is formed between two teachers who, for the purpose of this work, are able to regard themselves as true equals.

2. Both play roles at different times — observer and observed.

3. A series of observations is preceded by discussion as to objectives and needs. A brief for the observer is agreed, often limiting the scope of the observation to those objectives which seem to the observed to be most critical or significant.

4. After an observation, a discussion takes place and decisions are made about the tutoring during the next observations session. The intention is to try on each occasion to bring about *noticeable differences*.

Setting up such arrangements is not going to be easy. Timetables are rarely constructed with this kind of exercise in mind. However, it can be argued that, if the need is given high enough priority, then ways will be found.

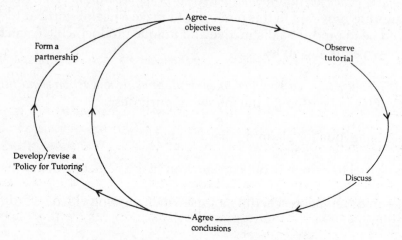

A system for the improvement of tutoring

Structured resources

What are structured resources?

These are the course books which form the core of the learning materials used by the student on SSS.

The functions of a course book are:

1. To give a comprehensive coverage of the subject matter with a minimum of extraneous detail.

2. To provide the student with a structure for the new learning.

3. To be sufficiently concise and compact to help the student when summarising or revising.

4. To be especially devoted to clarity so that the student can use it without the constant help and supervision of the teacher.

In the past, many teachers have rejected conventional textbooks when seeking suitable material for the independent student. They have argued that the text was too verbose and the content and style not near enough to the students' needs. This feeling has often led them into the task of producing all the resources needed for a course within the school, encouraged by the advances in technology which have removed many of the technical production problems.

Generally, it is better to avoid resource production if at all possible: there are too many other things that need doing. Exceptions could be made for very specialised topics and for local material. The other important exception is the preparation of student assignments.

So we are concerned mainly with the *search* for suitable material. Remember that there is no such thing as the perfect course book. You will certainly have to tailor your course book to fit your students' needs.

Here are a few general guidelines.

Generally prefer the small single topic book to the large comprehensive tome. This gives greater flexibility in organisation and is less threatening to the student. This may mean that your course will be based round a succession of small course books rather than a single text. Cost may, however, prove to be a problem.

Don't be too strongly influenced by the presence or absence of 'things to do'. The main purpose of the course book is to provide the structure of the new learning. You may find it better to design your own activities through the use of prepared assignments and the discussion in tutorials.

Generally prefer to buy or borrow course books rather than to produce your own core material.

Economise by buying in small sets rather than in class sets. This can be possible when you are operating a 'circus' and using small single topic books.

Evaluation check-list for structured resources

So what are the attributes of a good course book from the point of view of Supported Self-Study? Frankly, they are not very different from the attributes of any good textbook. Here is a check-list which may prove useful. You can use it to help in the evaluation of any course books, already possessed or in the process of being considered.

The underlying theme is *support*. Does the layout, design and content really support the learner who is working for part of the time independently?

Are these statements true about the course book that you are evaluating?

1. *The text is organised in small blocks, units or chapters.* Each learning task seems manageable. The end is in sight, not over some distant horizon. For younger and less able students, the shorter the better. A page at a time is often a useful principle.

2. *At the start of each block, there is a reasonable clear statement of the objectives for the block.* This need not (probably should not) be written according to some rigid formula derived from the theory of behavioural objectives. The simple question to ask is does the student get a clear picture of what knowledge and skills the block is aiming to teach?

---

3. *Throughout each block the structure is obvious and clear.* It will be made so by a well-designed system of headings and sub-headings. It should be possible to find your way easily during revision and to switch easily between a general overview and a more detailed consideration of one section.

4. *The sequencing of the information and ideas is helpful.* One step leads logically and easily to the next. There are no examples of knowledge being assumed before it has been given!

5. *The writing is concise and crisp.* This means that the sentences are short, the nouns concrete, the verbs active. There is no padding, no unnecessary academic jargon.

6. *The publishers have used typography carefully to aid clarity.* The skilful use of varied type sizes and the use of different kinds of type style can be very helpful.

7. *Visual images are used to help understanding.* This goes beyond simple illustration. A good course book uses diagrams to explain or reinforce ideas, thoroughly integrating the text with the images.

8. *The reading level is suitable for the target group.* This is an important test for the main course book but may not be so important for the enrichment resources.

9. *There are explicit arrangements for actively involving the learner.* This helps to maintain interest.

10. *There are self-assessment questions that are suitable for the self-study student.* These are another valuable aid to help the student to keep an active mind.

11. *There is a selection of assignments for teacher marking.*

12. *There is a list of useful references for additional work.*

13. *The whole package is attractive in appearance.*

You are unlikely to give an unreserved yes to every question; and some of the criteria will be more important to you than others. However, it is an exercise that is well worth doing.

Sources of structured resources

The commercial publishers

These will almost certainly be your main source. Standards have improved enormously in recent years and the best school textbooks are splendid as core material for Supported Self-Study. Many have been planned and designed with the more independent styles of learning in mind but, equally, many books which make no claims in this respect are often well worth consideration.

Obviously, the choice must be an individual one based on the criteria suggested above but also considering such matters as:

— subject matter being accurate and up to date;

— coverage right for the proposed course;

— style in keeping with the teacher's own preferred ways of presenting the subject.

The correspondence colleges

Some of the correspondence colleges offer their learning materials for use by institutions operating Open Learning systems. This is like the use of the Open University course units by other institutions working at degree level. There is already much experience of this in further education.

The course units cover a wide range of GCSE and A-level courses and there are also some units on basic skills.

The materials vary considerably in format and style. Some claim to be entirely self-contained; others make extensive reference to selected textbooks. Most make an attempt to match the requirements of a structured course for a student working alone. Of course, they were designed for adults and this should be borne in mind. However, some of the colleges are making a determined effort to enter the schools market and will welcome the co-operation of interested teachers.

A full list of correspondence colleges can be obtained from standard reference books like the Education Year Book.

Open Learning units

Open Learning in further education has concentrated heavily on resources. There are many production units and also a number of colleges acting as resource centres for their area. They can be very helpful to teachers seeking course materials in business and technical subjects.

'Self-study' books

There has been a spate of these in recent years and many of the commercial publishers have now entered this market. They are obviously responding to a demand and this is not only coming from mature learners. One publisher has recently extended its range to the younger age groups of the secondary school. The materials are varied, both in quality and style. Some are simply textbooks by another name. Others make a serious attempt to match the criteria for a structured course. Some include self-assessment tests. Many are simply listed as 'revision aids', giving essential information in note form with some practice questions. 'Model answers', 'Worked Examples' and multiple choice questions abound. Many would have to plead guilty to the charge that they concentrate too much on the skeleton, ignoring the flesh and blood. By themselves many of them would be unsatisfactory but they can often be usefully employed as part of a total package. The best are good by any standards. Here is a list of some of these materials which might be worth inspection.

Wiley's Programmed Texts
Teach Yourself Books (English Universities Press)
Made Simple Series (W H Allen)
Success Studybooks (John Murray)
Master Series (Macmillan)
M and E Handbooks (Macdonald and Evans)
Study Aids and Foundation Aids (Charles Letts)
Celtic Revision Aids
Breakthrough Series (Pan Books)
Linguaphone Language Courses
Audio-Forum Language Courses
Open University Course Units

Development projects and LEA resources units

These often have splendid material on specific topics. They are a good source of the small single topic books referred to above.

Some useful addresses

W H Allen
44 Hill Street, London W1X 8LB

Audio-Forum
31 Kensington Church Street, London W8 4LL

BBC Enterprises Ltd (film and video sales)
80 Wood Lane, London W12 0TT

British Leisure Publications
Windsor Court, East Grinstead House, East Grinstead, West Sussex RH19 1XA

Celtic Revision Aids
17-23 Nelson Way, Tuscam Trading Estate, Camberley, Surrey GU15 3EU

Guild Sound and Vision (film and video distributor)
6 Royce Road, Peterborough PE1 5YB

ILEA Learning Materials Service
Highbury Station Road, London N1D 1SB

International Correspondence Schools
341 Argyle Street, Glasgow G2 8LW

Isle of Wight Teachers' Centre
Upper St James Street, Newport, Isle of Wight PO30 1LQ

Kent Maths Project
West Kent Teachers' Centre, Deacon Court, Culverdon Park Road,
Tunbridge Wells TN4 9QX

Charles Letts
77 Borough Road, London SE1 1DW

Linguaphone Institute
209 Regent Street, London W1R 8AU

Longman Group Resources Unit
33-36 Tanner Row, York YO1 1TU

Macdonald and Evans
Estover Road, Estover, Plymouth, Devon PL6 7PZ

Macmillans
4 Little Essex Street, London WC2R 3LF

John Murray
50 Albermarle Street, London W1X 4BD

National Centre for School Technology
Trent Polytechnic, Burton Street, Nottingham NG1 4BU

National Extension College
18 Brooklands Avenue, Cambridge CB2 2HN

Open University Educational Enterprises
12 Cofferidge Close, Stony Stratford, Milton Keynes MK11 1BY

Pan Books
Cavaye Place, London SW10 9PG

Pitman's Correspondence College
Worcester Road, London SW19 7QQ

Rapid Results College
27/37 St George's Road, London SW19 4DS

Resources for Learning Development Unit
Bishopston School, Bishop Road, Bristol BS7 8LS

School Broadcasting Information (BBC)
Villiers House, The Broadway, Ealing, London W5 2PA

Tutor Tape Company Ltd
100 Great Russell Street, London WC1B 3LE

Wiley and Sons
Baffins Lane, Chichester, West Sussex PO19 1UD

Wolsey Hall
66 Banbury Road, Oxford OX2 6PR

Kinds and sources of enrichment resources

First some important principles for enrichment resources.

1. Seek material that is *rich* in data or stimulation. Don't insist that the items fit exactly with the needs of your students. Don't expect enrichment resources to provide the structure and guidance that the learner needs. Instead, choose these resources for their variety, interest and stimulation. Much of the excitement of resource-based learning is in the seeking and finding of relevant information and ideas from the *raw data of the real world*.

2. Prefer resources that are small in format — the little booklet, the single sheet, the short tape or filmstrip. They will be economic in use and sharply focused on the learning tasks.

3. Don't attempt to make your own resources, except for very local or special needs. If resources have to be produced locally, then try to join some co-operative activity so that the work is shared.

4. Get the support of the librarian and library service as early as possible. This means always, as a matter of routine, involving the school librarian at the planning stage of any learning programme. The librarian can, at the outset, usually make valuable suggestions about the availability of resources which can influence the objectives and style of the whole programme. In addition, when the librarian is fully aware of the developments that are taking place in a department, you have trained eyes and ears constantly on the look-out for additional material.

5. Look widely — new media; resources outside the school; other people.

Here is a quick reminder of the likely sources:

★   Commercial publishers;

★   Development projects (national, LEA, training institutions);

★   LEA support services such as resource centres, school library services, museum services, teachers' centres;

★　Broadcasting authorities;

★　Audio-visual producers;

★　Computer software producers;

★　Industrial, commercial and professional bodies.

Get it free if you can! If not, borrow it! And when you have to pay for something, prefer to buy in small sets rather than in class sets.

Wherever possible, leave these kinds of resources for the library to acquire, store and maintain; but make sure that you understand the storage and retrieval system. A separate departmental system involves a lot of work. Some departments prefer to collect their enrichment resources into packages for each module of the learning programme. This will be described in the pages dealing with assignments.

Organising a collection of enrichment resources

Most subject departments have their own collections of enrichment resources. Some prefer to keep as much as possible directly under their own control; others believe that there are practical advantages and sound educational reasons for relying on the school library. Whatever the choice, some kind of system needs to operate within the department. There are two main options:

1.　Set up a full storage and retrieval system for all the department resources and train the students to use it properly. This is necessary for a large collection. It involves a lot of work; some help and advice from the librarian might be forthcoming.

2.　Operate a *very simple* system for essential resources only. Those on a given unit of study are kept together so they can be wheeled out when a class is working on that unit. Within each unit collection, each item is numbered as it is acquired (an acquisition number system!). Therefore the numbers themselves don't mean anything, they are simply a convenient short way of referring to items (item number 34, item number 102). You will need to keep a list of names and item numbers (like a list of telephone numbers).

There is a lot to be said for the second simple system. It is easy to set up and maintain, and the students will find it easy to use. However, it assumes that the quantity of enrichment material kept in the department is small, that the unit basis of organisation is acceptable and that the library is able to provide a good additional service to provide a much wider range of enrichment resources.

Many departments that operate simple systems for their enrichment resources make heavy use of the fibreboard open magazine files which are available from library suppliers. These can be numbered in the way described above. They are excellent for the storage of a variety of resources — books, topic booklets, cuttings, single photographs, audio tapes, sets of slides, and so on. The result is a mini-library to serve the needs of the particular unit of study.

Assignments

An introduction to assignments

In Supported Self-Study, the student receives guidance from three sources:

— from the tutorial with the teacher;

— from the main structured course;

— from assignments prepared by the teacher.

The first of these is the most important and no Supported Self-Study should be undertaken without a careful set of arrangements for tutorials.

Where the tutorial arrangements are good and the main structured course is helpful in its guidance to students, the need for assignments may be slight.

However, assignments are absolutely essential where a wide range of unstructured resources is being used. In this situation, the assignments provide the guidance, set the tasks, pose the problems; while the resources serve simply as raw material.

There are also some definite advantages in the use of prepared assignments:

1. Your well-prepared assignments provide the best way of differentiating for individual abilities, needs and interests.

2. It is easier to produce a number of different assignments to respond to individual needs, rather than trying to adapt or rewrite the resources.

3. Assignments encourage greater flexibility in your use of resources. One resource item can be used by many different assignments, in different parts of a course and for different purposes. Contrast this with the inflexibility of the resource item which has detailed instructions, tasks, etc built in.

Designing a system for assignments

Assignments are usually written on single sheets of A4 or A5 paper or card. Like the resources, they can simply be numbered or lettered for quick and easy reference (Assignment 2, Assignment 24, etc). Then store them in a card index file (A5) or a filing cabinet (A4) and they can be retrieved quickly. Again, there is no meaning attached to the numbers. They are (like telephone numbers) just a quick and easy reference system.

A good assignments system will mean the creation of a large number of assignments. You have not only to cover all the topics within the learning programme but also to provide alternative assignments for different needs, interests and abilities. So you need to have a flow chart showing the relationship of the assignments to each other, in terms of sequence, level of difficulty, and so on.

Opposite is an example of such a flow chart with a key to the conventional symbols adopted. It provides the teacher with an instant view of the structure and sequence of the whole topic, and demonstrates the options available. Of course, there is nothing sacred about the symbols and meanings used here. This is merely a model to help a department get started on its own thinking.

Writing assignments

This is not easy but the effort involved usually pays handsome dividends.

The following are the jobs that an assignment aims to do.

1. *Provide a good title and clear objectives for the task.* This gives an advance view of the task. It can give an outline of the subject matter and also an indication of the skills which will be developed. It is best to avoid the jargon of educational objectives; explain it all in commonsense, practical language.

2. *Give details of the resources to be used.* If there is a main course book, your assignment should give advice as to which sections are to be used and sometimes as to which sections should be missed out. It will also need to refer to other enrichment resources. There is a difficulty here: should you prescribe, or should you suggest, or should you leave the students to make their own decisions? There is no simple single answer; it must depend on a number of things. To what extent are the students capable of making their own decisions? Does the unit of study lend itself to different individual approaches? Or does it demand a fairly standard and uniform response? So the guidance given in the assignment may be prescriptive, or open-ended, or, most likely of all, a mixture of both. In making these decisions, the teacher will always have in mind the main aim of SSS of developing student responsibility. So there is a lot to be said for adopting a forward-looking approach rather than being too cautious.

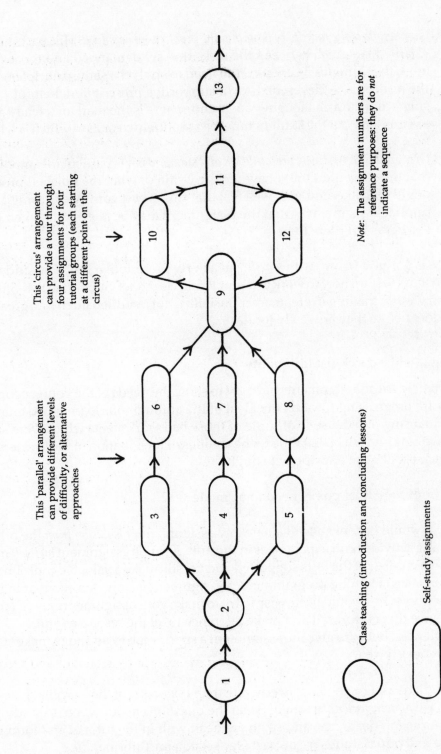

This 'circus' arrangement can provide a tour through four assignments for four tutorial groups (each starting at a different point on the circus)

This 'parallel' arrangement can provide different levels of difficulty, or alternative approaches

Note: The assignment numbers are for reference purposes: they do *not* indicate a sequence

Class teaching (introduction and concluding lessons)

Self-study assignments

An assignment system

3. *Give details of the tasks to be done and the problems to be solved.* This part should clearly distinguish between the tasks that are demanded and those that are at the student's discretion. You need to apply the same principles as for the resources. A clever mixture of supportive prescription, helpful suggestion and challenging open-endedness is the mark of a really good assignment. But the student must be absolutely clear as to which is which.

4. *Give guidance on styles, presentation and standards.* It is particularly important that the students should have a clear vision of what the finished product might look like. You may well feel that this is best conveyed during a tutorial but remember that the assignment may be referred to when the teacher is not there to help.

There is nothing wrong with *starting* in a fairly prescriptive way. The students' first need is to learn how to work to a simple and clear brief. Supported Self-Study is a *progressive* training in greater responsibility, not a sudden lurch into greater freedom before they are ready for it.

Assignments: check-list for quality

Ultimately, these assignments have got to serve the needs of the young people who are progressing towards the ideal of the autonomous learner. We must avoid lapsing into the style of some of those bad worksheets which were so uninspiring and which left little to the abilities or imagination of the learners. So a check-list like the one opposite might help.

Two important final points need to be made.

First, it would be foolish to evaluate any assignment *in isolation from* the other learning activities and experiences in the unit. A single assignment *by itself* may fail on a number of the tests suggested and yet still make a valuable contribution to a balanced learning programme. An assignment is only one element in the programme. You would be unwise to try to make your assignments give *all* the guidance that is required and make reference to all the resources and experiences. Better to give the assignment a specific job to do and to make sure that it does it well.

Second, the assignment is concerned with the *substance* of the learning. It does not have a *management* function. So all the questions about where to study, use of equipment, deadlines, and so on are dealt with in the tutorial and form part of the individual student's contract (see section on Tutoring).

1. Avoid the fact-extraction/fact-reproduction type of task. Let us be certain that we are not simply asking them to transfer information from books into their notes (without them having to think about it at all!).

2. Make sure that the students' thinking skills are used. Get them to *select* from data, analyse it and prepare it for presentation for a particular purpose.

3. Remember in all subjects to encourage imaginative thinking as well as the purely analytical.

4. Make demands on the students' organising skills.

5. Promote student decision making.

6. Check the language carefully. It must be concise and *well within* the students' capability. This latter point is important. It ensures that, when they are engaged in self-study, the queries concerning the meaning or interpretation of the assignment are kept to a minimum.

7. Make sure that they have a clear vision of what the end-product might look like. Sometimes it helps for students to see good examples of work done by students who have previously tackled the assignment; or you might show a few possible outcomes in outline form only. Once again, we have the dilemma of how to give maximum support and guidance without at the same time taking away all initiative from the learner. As always, success follows a balanced approach.

8. Use models to suggest ways of tackling the task.

9. Keep notes about the assignments in use. They will certainly need modifying.

An example of an assignment

THE MEDIEVAL TOWN

What was it like living in a medieval town? That is the question for you to answer. You will have to search for evidence and then sort it out to make an interesting presentation.

Use your course book as the main guide. But also consult items 23, 24, 28 (audio-tape), 29, 31 and 35 (set of slides). You should also refer back to your own work on the two previous assignments as well as your worksheets completed on the town trail.

We will discuss in tutorial how you might research some special topics in the library. The librarian is well prepared to give you advice and assistance.

Your task is simply to collect as much information as you can and then prepare to present it in one of these ways:

1. You can write a diary of a person of your own age for a whole week in a year that you choose.

2. You can prepare an illustrated newspaper of several pages for a date that you choose.

3. You can propose at tutorial to make a different presentation of your own choosing.

Whatever you decide to do these are helpful hints.

1. Make it real by describing *in detail*. Keep asking yourself questions. What did it really look like? How would it really have happened?

2. Remember *all* the senses — sight, sound, smell, taste and touch.

3. Don't just give the facts. Give some idea of how did it *feel* to be alive at that time. Appeal to your reader's heart as well as his head.

We shall look at some work already done by other students during tutorial and that will help you to decide your own approach.

A short bibliography

The following books have been chosen because they could be of *practical* help to the teacher who is setting up a Supported Self-Study scheme.

Beckett, L, *Maintaining Choice in the Secondary Curriculum* (Working Paper 20), CET, 1981.

This was one of CET's earlier investigations into the possibilities of Supported Self-Study as a contribution to the problems of falling rolls in secondary schools.

Lewis, R (Ed), *Open Learning Guides*, CET, 1984-86.
   1. Open Learning in Action
   2. How to Help Learners Assess Their Progress
   3. How to Tutor and Support Learners
   4. What is Open Learning?
   5. How to Develop and Manage an Open Learning Scheme
   6. How to Communicate with the Learner
   7. How to Manage the Production Process
   8. How to Find and Adapt Materials and Select Media

These may be of help especially for those teachers who are planning work with older students. The focus is on further education and open learning.

Marland, M, *Schools Council Curriculum Bulletin 9: Information Skills in the Secondary Curriculum*, Methuen Educational, 1981.

This is a most helpful book. It offers a practical approach to all learning tasks. Well worth studying.

Miller, J C, *Tutoring: the Guidance and Counselling Role of the Tutor in Vocational Preparation*, FEU, 1982.

Although this book is more about counselling than about academic tutoring, it is an excellent summary of some important principles.

Rainbow, R, *Making Supported Self-Study Work: the Holyrood School experience*, CET, 1987.

A first-class account of work in one secondary school.

Thomas, J B, *The Self in Education*, NFER, 1980.

This is a clear and helpful summary of research into the theories and principles underlying Supported Self-Study.

Waterhouse, P, *Managing the Learning Process*, McGraw Hill, 1983.

This is a practical handbook of classroom management. It focuses on individual and small group work, with a strong emphasis on the role of the teacher as manager. Very useful for teachers undertaking work with large lower school classes.

Waterhouse, P, *Supported Self-Study in Secondary Education* (Working Paper 24), CET, 1983.

This was written at the end of phase 1 of the CET Project. It sets out the possibilities for the school and for the local authority but it is not a 'how to do it' handbook.

Index